Help for Parents of a Handicapped Child

Help for Parents of a Handicapped Child

Nancy Roberts

Concordia Publishing House
St. Louis

Copyright © 1981
Concordia Publishing House
3558 South Jefferson Avenue
St. Louis, Missouri 63118
Manufactured in the United States of America

1 2 3 4 5 6 7 8 9 10 WP 90 89 88 87 86 85 84 83 82 81

Library of Congress Cataloging in Publication Data

Roberts, Nancy, 1924—
    Help for parents of a handicapped child.

    (Coping with trauma series)
    1. Developmentally disabled children—Family relationships. 2. Handi-
capped children—Family relationships. I. Title II. Series.
HV891.R6   649′.1528   81-1830
ISBN 0-570-08254-4   AACR2

So faith, hope, love abide, these three;
but the greatest of these is love.
1 Corinthians 13:13

Contents

Acknowledgments

I want to thank the families who have shared so openly with me. Their feelings and insights as helpers have come through years of pain and pleasure, prayer and perseverance.

Each person has given something of their own courage seasoned with an abundant measure of faith.

Dr. Olson Huff has contributed both Christian compassion and professional guidance gained through the years of treating children who have disabilities. His help and observations have been invaluable, for he has a unique dedication to the problems of helping parents as well as his patients.

Jimmy D. Brown, a counselor at North Carolina Vocational Rehabilitation, has been a source of encouragement and genuine spiritual inspiration. I am grateful for the cases he has suggested as well as for his creative ability in commenting on points worthy of including in this project.

The support of these people makes this book their book, too!

Foreword

One of your loved ones is crying for help. And you, as you offer help, are crying too. Willing as you may be to stand by faithfully and lovingly, you are nevertheless on duty 24 hours a day, 7 days a week, in a setting not of your own choosing or making.

Apart from occasional visits and offers of assistance from others, the daily burden of care falls on you. It doesn't take long before your resources are drained and you cry for relief. If only someone could spell you now and then, if only someone understood your special needs. It's not that you want to abandon your station at the side of your loved one, but even those who care for patients grow weary and dispirited. The helper needs help too.

This booklet, written by someone in a position similar to yours, is intended to offer you encouragement, support, and suggestions for outside assistance and understanding. It means to lift your eyes to your ever-present Helper and to open up avenues of communication with counselors and others in like circumstances.

Your cries for help have been heard.

—The Publisher

Introduction

I have often asked myself, What is the most important thing for the helper of the retarded or developmentally disabled person to do?

Over the years I have found that first of all the helper must honestly accept reality and work within it to achieve the most that can be achieved with that special person's life.

It is continued involvement with that person as a person. There must be orientation that the entire family is a part of, an orientation realistically based, not expecting this person to be like someone else—normal, whatever normal is—but expecting that person to be the most independent individual he or she is capable of being. Honest acceptance and making the person as independent as possible are the two basic ingredients of the normalcy of the marriage, the family, and the life of the helper or helpers.

It is the belief that a person's value is based upon God's acceptance of him/her as a soul as unique and precious to Him as our own soul, and that it is no less important because the person has a disability or a special need. One of the mistakes we have traditionally made is that a person's value is based primarily upon his or her ability to succeed. God tells us consistently that this is not so, that the value is the person and is not based upon intellect, physical prowess, or normalcy of mind or body.

The developmentally disabled person's need of salvation and redemption is the same as our own, and their salvation and redemption comes the same way ours does: God has given it to us and we reach out and accept it regardless of our mental age.

I think that for many people who sustain the handicapped or those unable to conceptualize as we do, this has been a gray area. We have been so inculcated with the idea that unless we can fully understand all the nuances of doctrine or talk with God or intellectualize, we cannot be saved.

I truly believe that persons with special needs, who may not even be able to verbalize their relationship to God within themselves, are unique and precious. Their redemption needs to be affirmed like anyone else's.

Realistic expectations, teaching independence, belief in the worth of the disabled person, and actualizing their preciousness to God are all ideals which the helper will seek to realize.

Olson Huff, M.D.
Developmental Pediatrician
Developmental Evaluation Center,
Asheville, N.C.

1
They Couldn't Tell Me Why . . . .

Bobby's mother, Janice, is an attractive brunette with lovely eyes and a warm smile, but beneath her careful composure you sense an almost unbearable strain.

"At Bobby's birth we were told we had a fine, healthy boy. About a year and a half later he appeared to have a seizure. His doctor said he could see no evidence of anything wrong and would have to observe him during a seizure. Later a spastic twitching developed in his face and then in his movements.

"I wasn't able to find out anything from the doctor and decided to take him to the health center. They did an evaluation and told me he was retarded. I just fell apart. I felt as if I could have died. I was in tears. The lady spoke very harshly to me. 'Mrs. Martin,' she said, 'you've got to get yourself together. You are just going to have to face up to it, your boy is retarded, and you're going to have to live with it for the rest of your life.' Her manner was abrupt and clinical.

"It was very hard for me to accept this in just five minutes. When I asked her what was wrong with him and why, she couldn't give me an answer. My husband came over to the health center and met me. He didn't believe anything was wrong either. 'They just can't prove this to me,' I said. We went outside in the rain, and I was crying. He didn't put his arm around me or anything but simply said, 'Well, I have to get back to work,' and he walked away. Our problems started right then. My husband was a perfectionist and blamed me for the baby's being born this way. If I hadn't had God, I wouldn't have had anything. I became wrapped up in Bobby's care and needs. My husband, on the other hand, had always been very involved in his work and in the National Guard, and they were most important to him. Three years later we were divorced.

"As Bobby grew older he began to give me problems. It was very hard for me to work. No one wanted to take care of him. He was often sent home from school for temper outbursts and aggressive behavior. I couldn't even earn money by taking care of children in my home because other parents thought Bobby would give them his bad habits.

"Finally, I was able to make an appointment for Bobby with a pediatrician who specialized in developmental disabilities. He diagnosed Bobby as hyperactive and put him on a new medication that is now helping him some. But the most important thing has been that this doctor has really listened to me and cared about my problem.

"I have really felt heartsick for Bobby since the divorce. My former husband would come to take the two normal children out, but not Bobby. He would have his bag all packed, and my husband would come and leave him each time. The center here told Bobby, 'Your father doesn't want you,' and then they said to me, 'He has to be realistic.' I think that's pretty much for a retarded youngster to take.

"Sometimes I have had to live on welfare, and it has been very humiliating. My former husband is vice-president of a company and makes very good money. He says I'm using Bobby as a crutch to avoid work, but Bobby has been out of school so much no employer would put up with my being out so often. One teacher wrote me letters about him almost every day. She wanted to lock him up in a tiny padded room they have at the school. My pediatrician says Bobby lives in a little world of fear within himself, and I'm afraid this would damage him even more.

"During Bobby's kindergarten years, the mother's group helped me a lot, and one kindergarten teacher took me aside and talked to me until she talked me out of being depressed. 'You need counseling from someone at mental health,' she told me. But I just looked around me and saw other people dealing with this and felt if they could, I could too. When I became depressed, it helped to get busy. One of the reasons I felt so alone was because my parents would say, 'Nothing's wrong with our Bobby. God will heal him.' That made me feel as if no one close to me understood the problem. For awhile I felt hostile toward God for letting this happen.

"It seems now that it may have been the obstetrician's fault. Bobby was ready to be born before I got to the delivery room, and there was a wait before I could be taken in. Perhaps the cord was around his neck too long. My own obstetrician could not be located, and a co-worker delivered the baby.

"It has been twelve years now since Bobby was born, and I would love to have him just like he is for me, but for him I wish he were normal. By this I mean he is a very affectionate and loving child, very caring, and I feel he is probably giving me more love than my other two ever will. Sometimes his teachers have real behavior problems with him, and last year he attacked one of them; but I have good control over him.

"Bobby is potty trained and eats by himself, but he needs some help with dressing and with brushing his teeth. The respite care program has been a real blessing, for it is the only program that offers me any relief or a chance to occasionally do some of the things I would like to do.

"I feel very sad and frustrated at times over the conflict with my 12- and 14-year-old children that is caused by Bobby's behavior. They are always screaming, 'Bobby's in my room,' or 'Get Bobby out of here.' It is not easy for them to adjust. Mostly he plays alone.

"My advice to other parents would be: try to stay close to God, be strong, keep busy, and talk to other people with similar problems. By all means don't allow yourself to become isolated. Keep up with things to help your child at school. Parents have to stick together to get things through for these children. One can't do it alone, but a group can. And by all means stay abreast of what the Association for Retarded Citizens is doing."

2
Attitudes of
the Helper

A helper is someone like you or me who helps another human being function and, in the most basic sense, sustain life.

This booklet deals with the attitudes and problems you may have as a helper. All too often professional attention has been focused purely on the needs of the individual with the affliction, which may be retardation, a learning disability, or a physical impairment.

In many cases your entire family will become a supportive network, and it is important that their lives are not distorted by the situation and that their needs are also recognized. Perhaps you have willingly assumed this obligation through marriage to such a person. On the other hand, you may be assuming this role with real apprehension after the birth of a retarded or learning-disabled infant.

In any event, you as a helper must first deal with reality. You are not dealing with a crisis that will pass, but with a situation that will be a continuing one for the lifetime of the impaired person. The expectation we all have when a child is conceived and a pregnancy carried out is that the child is going to be normal. If the infant is abnormal instead, there is severe shock and the necessity of facing the overwhelming sense of loss that occurs when what was anticipated does not happen.

Parents as well as the entire family suffer from real grief. Since your grief does not have the finality of death, ministers, friends, and even professionals are often unable to give the comfort and support you expect. The same reactions we have toward death are normal and the stages are similar. You may go through a period of denial: you refuse to believe that anything is wrong with your child; a period of bargaining, in which you may plead with God, "If you will only make this child whole, Lord, I promise to be a better Christian."

Anger is another normal reaction, but finally, if you are to function in a healthy fashion, there must be acceptance. Hopefully, those who are trying to help you will be aware of these stages, for they are actually grief at work and part of your path toward adjustment.

It may come as a surprise that your child's physician will also grieve, for he has had his own expectations for this child. Your physician experiences feelings of keen disappointment and frustration that he must handle, for doctors are cure oriented. You and your doctor are probably struggling with some of the same emotions.

Sometimes the professional is faced with the problem of total denial on the part of the helper or parents. You will make it much harder for yourself and your physician if you take this attitude. The professional should give you the facts as honestly and simply as possible. No one is served in the long run by not being completely truthful. If the situation is not explained fully, your trust in the professional will suffer.

You must have full confidence in the physician or other professional in order to work through your own feelings and sustain the person you will be helping. The first weeks and months after you learn of the situation are frequently a period of some depression and an abnormal amount of fatigue. You may feel emotionally drained and depleted. This is a natural consequence of grief and shock. Like any serious disappointment or heartbreak in life, how soon and how well you begin to mend depends upon you. In my own experience, I have found a source of help which I hope you will seek. It is the Holy Spirit.

One of the wondrous attributes of the Holy Spirit is inner healing. It is not mentioned often enough in the church today. Martin Luther's words continue to ring down through the centuries, saying, "They are truly beautiful proclaimers of Easter, but shameful preachers of Pentecost. . . . Christ has earned for us not only God's mercy but also the gift of the

Holy Spirit. . . . A Christian should have the Holy Spirit and lead a new life, or know that he has not received Christ at all."

The gift of the Holy Spirit truly infuses us with "new life." Your part is to admit the "dryness" and the discouragement, open yourself, and accept by faith the gift Jesus promised to give you. A simple prayer will enable you to receive the strength and love of the Holy Spirit in your own life.

You must not expect your experience in the Holy Spirit to be like anyone else's. Jesus deals with us as individuals. Some experience exultant joy and a sense of His presence, others find a quiet peace, and someone else may have a sense of uncertainty as to whether anything has happened at all, but it has.

When a seed falls upon the ground in a forest, it does so without the clatter of cymbals. The earth receives the gift of the seed quietly and begins to nourish it as it has done for untold ages. Thus the Holy Spirit begins to grow in you. The attitudes of the helper who receives this gift will begin to express love, joy, wisdom, and new life.

Can you imagine how much these qualities in you will aid the person you wish to help?

Most of us have been influenced by myths of a typical American family, our expectations fed by movies or television. There are few programs that center around a family with an abnormal child or around a person with any sort of disability. If you have an opportunity, you may wish to see the movies *Joni* or *Best Boy*. It helps to know that situations involving abnormalities can be faced with courage.

You can be sure you have not been singled out by the Lord for punishment, and if you will take a closer look at the lives around you, you will find few of them that have not been touched by similar problems.

It is important that you find the right professional, most often a physician but sometimes your pastor, who has knowledge and compassion in the area of your situation. You need someone who will encourage you to express your emotions and the struggle that is going on within you and your family as you move toward acceptance. There are times of stress, frustration, and rebellion, and it is essential that you find someone with whom you can discuss these reactions honestly.

Many people with retarded children are tempted to feel, and to a degree, rightly, that a person does not fully understand unless they have a retarded child or a disabled person in their family. This is true if we seek complete understanding, but even those of us with retarded children often disagree, and understanding is imperfect.

One family will accept behavior that another would not permit. One may take a child everywhere, but others do not understand this and for them occasional trips or outings without the person they are caring for may be essential. You may find considerable comfort in simply talking or praying with a friend who does not share this problem but is devoutly Christian.

For some of you a mother's group that meets regularly provides encouragement and an opportunity to share the more unique feelings of those who are parents and helpers of a retarded child. When husbands and wives divide into separate groups, they may feel freer to express themselves.

It is not unusual for men to have feelings of guilt, embarrassment, and wounded pride when they become the father of an infant with some abnormality. Although these ideas have no validity or foundation in medical fact, they are still present, and men need an opportunity to share them with other men. In many cases the father has never confronted his emotions. He may believe the problem was somehow caused by something in his own heritage, a lack of consideration for his wife, a secret sin, or is even a reflection upon his virility. These are psychological problems that, if not thoroughly resolved by sound counseling, will damage the marital relationship. Many churches have combined their financial resources to support a Christian family-counseling service. Where this is not available, you will want to contact the mental health department or a private counselor your pastor recommends.

All too often Exodus 34:7 surfaces in our minds: "God will by no means clear the guilty, visiting the iniquity upon the children and the children's children, to the third and fourth generation." When we read this we may cringe inside and ask ourselves, What terrible thing exists in the background of our families, or in me, to have caused this? A verse like this brings self-pity, depression, and despair, the very antithesis of the Lord's will for you in your situation.

Instead we must claim Jeremiah 31:34: "I will forgive their iniquity, and I will remember their sin no more." There is not one of us whose ancestors have been free of the stain of sin, but here is assurance that the Lord is able to recompense or compensate for these sins in later generations. If this continues to trouble you, I suggest purchasing a copy of *Nave's Topical Bible* and reading often the section on the forgiveness of sin. There are more than enough beautiful verses on God's forgiveness to reassure us.

We do know that drug addiction may result in problems for new-born children and that certain other diseases may be transmitted through the parents to an unborn infant. But many disabilities are the result of some birth injury or deprivation despite the character of the child's parents and the best efforts of the attending physician. The probability of an abnormal child increases when certain factors are present, but it can also happen without them. Certainly, we may wish to obtain genetic counseling after the birth of a Down's syndrome child, but this need not discourage us from having other children.

It is important to remember that retarded or learning-disabled children, just as those who later become impaired through disease or accident, occur in truly Christian families as well as in those that profess no religion. We cannot consider this as a punishment. Those who have parented such children find they bring with them deep insights in tenderness and love.

Absolutely nothing is achieved by a continuing obsession with the cause of a handicap that cannot be readily diagnosed. We would be draining ourselves and wasting valuable time.

You must now ask yourself, What can love and patience accomplish? What is the best possible diet, stimulation, exercise? What can you do to assist this individual in developing his or her highest potential? This is your challenge.

Limitations and potential will, to an amazing degree, depend on your attitude as the helper. If you have certain limitations in your mind beyond which you feel this person will never go, they will seldom progress beyond them. Continuing to set goals and patiently encouraging and assisting progress toward them is the way miracles happen.

3
Needs of the Helper

Your needs as a helper might first appear to be complex or unique. On the contrary, they are the normal needs of every human being. There is real danger that when normal needs are not met, the helper will begin to feel drained or even give up entirely.

In almost every case the love of the helper for the person he or she is sustaining is tender and deep. There is great loyalty and dedication toward supporting another, often the investment of much of one's own life.

Unfortunately, individuals receiving this support may without realizing it become so demanding and possessive that the helpers are prevented from having any life of their own. The disabled person depends on them not only for physical care and assistance but for companionship, entertainment, stimulation, everything. They become resentful if their helper has any outside activity: pleasure, relaxation, friends, or even a quiet time alone.

This works as great a strain upon the relationship of helper and helped one as it would upon a marriage relationship, a friendship, or any other human interaction. No matter how devoted you are to another person, you need time for yourself if you are to maintain your mental and emotional health. Therefore, it is vitally necessary to make every effort to explain this whenever possible and resist the demands upon time that you rightfully feel you need for yourself and would have in the average family or home environment.

Handicapped persons do not always realize that the Lord has placed an obligation to be more unselfish not simply upon the helper but upon them too. They expect this quality in the helper, but it has not always occurred to them to examine their own behavior, expectations, and requests. The happy, normal relationship is never a smothering one or one where our entire life is lived vicariously through another. If this is happening to you as a helper, you may be courting an emotional breakdown and encouraging a situation that eventually may become intolerable.

There is wisdom in the saying that it takes two to make a marriage. It also takes two to produce an unhealthy situation—the victimizer and the person who allows himself or herself to become the victim.

When you love someone and feel a sense of responsibility for them, how do you retain your sense of well-being, which really makes you a *better* helper? How do you keep from being victimized?

Even the retarded person and the disabled quickly learn methods of manipulating the people around them. It begins as a way of communicating normal and reasonable needs. But requests may assume unreasonable, even irrational proportions unless limits are placed upon them.

You say you want to do these things for someone you love, but do you want to do things that will ultimately make them more dependent? Do you want to cater to whims and give in to requests that come when you are physically and emotionally depleted? You are confirming habit patterns that are the road to martyrdom for you and will result in less self-reliance and growth for them.

Each time you give in to demands you know are unreasonable without pointing out your opinion and refusing, you may be storing away emotions of strong resentment within yourself. This is not being unselfish; it is being weak, and it is a course that often leads us to explode with accumulated frustration and anger. Most frightening of all, you are taking a course that may one day tempt you to throw up your hands and walk out on the entire situation—a shattering occasion both for you and the person whom you love.

How can you prevent this? The first step is to begin to

inwardly ask yourself some questions about the sort of requests and demands you are receiving. Write them down and place a check against those things you find particularly irrational or irritating. Now, which should be firmly but kindly refused because they are unnecessary or because they foster undue dependence upon you? Begin by saying no to at least one or two of them.

Vague, diffused feelings or just hoping for change is of no use. You must try to define for yourself what areas in the helping relationship are the sources of the most acute strain and irritation. Write down whether you feel you need more time for yourself, what you would like to do with it, and whether it is even remotely practical in terms of time and budget.

Would you like to take a class? Would you like to lunch with a friend occasionally? Spend some free time on a craft each week? Go to church more often, swim or bowl weekly? You may need classes in assertiveness to carry out your decisions. Just being able to say "I need to get out of the house for awhile" can be important.

Do you feel guilty about this? The prophets sought places where they might be alone to think and pray. Christ felt this same need. It is an abnormal person rather than a normal one who must constantly be in someone's company or insist on spending every minute with a loved one. Gibran, in *The Prophet*, puts it thus:

". . . . Let there be spaces in your togetherness,
And let the winds of the heavens dance between
you.
Love one another, but make not a bond of love:
Let it rather be a moving sea between the shores of
your souls."

There is something about this time apart that brings inner renewal to the helper and even the ability to better minister to another person.

4
Understanding Limitations and Potential

A natural longing on the part of parents and helpers of a person with a disability is to search for a crystal ball. What will this person be like 10 years from now or 20? What will his or her limitations be? How great is the potential for something approaching normalcy?

These questions can be a form of torture, and in most respects they simply are a waste of time and emotional energy. Even those with the same IQ or the same disability will differ from each other in achievements and independence. We do not know all the reasons, but the love and faith of the helper is vitally important as a determining factor in progress and performance.

We cannot always predict future achievement but it's encouraging to talk with someone like Jerry Massey, the director of the Nevins Center, a sheltered workshop in Charlotte, N. C.

"Richard came here when he was about twenty, and according to the system he had reached his potential," says Massey. "He had been through special education in the school system, but without a lot of progress. He had been ridiculed in a high school that included his class but was for normal boys and girls. When he came here, he grew interested in adult education and in adjusting more socially. The greatest thing we had going for us was that the parents were with us all the way.

"He really began to shine in the Special Olympics program, and another important incentive was his interest in obtaining his driver's license. He did so well in sports that he ended up participating in the Winter Special Olympics at Showboat, Colo. The support of the community, the fund-raising events gave him a good feeling.

"Today, Richard has his own car, drives to and from work and hasn't had any accidents. He's wheeling around in Lincolns and Cadillacs, etc., all day because his job at an auto upholstery shop involves picking up the cars and returning them.

"It is hard to pinpoint Richard's problem and give it a name. We only know that he was damaged at birth and was always slower than other children. In the regular school system he was deprived and singled out in an unfortunate way. He did not have those feelings of rejection here at the sheltered workshop.

"But the goal was always to place him in a normal society. His IQ had tested at about 70 to 75, but the most important thing was whether he could do the job. I think the assimilation into the real world is best because I believe the public must realize and accept that here is a person with wants, needs, abilities, and dreams.

"When he came to the workshop, he was not outgoing, and suddenly he's out here and allowed to be a person. He began interacting with people and became the sort of fellow that the other boys looked up to. He formed some normal friendships with other young men and started dating as well. He lives at home, and his parents still give him financial advice.

"We have one girl who went through the special-education system at the center for our trainable mentally retarded. I think we have finally found for her the sort of work she likes. Most of the jobs at our workshop are assembling and packaging. For quite awhile we had a real problem with her because she disliked a sedentary type job very much.

"Now we are doing a very simple operation called shingles on a stick. We put the stick in a jig and attach shingles to it with a pneumatic staple gun. For the first time Ann has a job that keeps her up and walking because she's the person who opens the bundles of shingles and helps put them out for the workers. She will also stack the finished shingle stick. It is a joy to watch her putting energy to work that was a problem for her before we were able to channel it. Ann has an IQ of about 55 and is a happy, cooperative person.

"We are especially proud of Marie. She came here from the state institution and was placed in group home living. She did so well that she has now been moved into an apartment that she shares with another girl. She rides the city bus from the apartment to the workshop, and sometimes things happen that make her ashamed to be with the others. She has complained about one young man who pulls the bus cord to tease the driver. When she first came out of the institution, she wouldn't have thought of complaining.

"A pretty girl, who looks like Julie Andrews, Marie inspects telephone transmitters. She checks them for the proper date, as certain years are rejects. She has her own circle of friends with IQs in the mid-sixties. We envision for her an outside situation, perhaps as a PBX operator or even in a plant where she could be seated and work in a lab or on an assembly line of almost any kind. Marie wears leg braces because of a birth problem and can go here or there but cannot stand for long periods. Unfortunately, most businesses with assembly lines are in outlying areas without bus service.

"It has discouraged me but I realize that sometime in the next six months we will find the right thing for her. She has some social life through a nearby community college after hours program. Occasionally, they take three boys and three girls to the movies or dinner. There should be a group here that would do more than this, as it is a rotation situation. Of the 165 in the workshop, probably 60 percent have little or no recreational contact on the outside."

Marie has been at the workshop for seven years, and never during this time does Massey remember meeting either of her parents. In this situation the helpers have disappeared and the public has taken over the responsibility.

There are other familiar situations, according to Massey.

"It was not until she was in her mid to late 40s that Vera came to us," he says. "She could talk but was very withdrawn. Love and stimulation were almost totally lacking in her home situation. We kept working with her. At first she wouldn't even go to the cafeteria and eat lunch. Then we got her in there but she would eat with her back to everyone else. She was always clean but would have on about four or five sets of clothing. Vera would never go to any of the dances, saying it was against her religious beliefs.

"We kept moving her desk in the workshop closer and closer to the cafeteria door; then, finally, she was standing in line like everyone else. She was living with an aged aunt, and at home she had not even been allowed to eat at the table with other people. This woman had almost become a closet case, when with love and stimuli she might have tested in the 60s. The helper in the home environment has been a negative one.

"I only wish we had enough group homes and apartments under supervision. So many of these people do not need to be in institutions, for they are capable of semi-independent living and of so much more development.

"One of the saddest experiences for me is to see a young adult whose parents still will not accept a disability. They will say, 'My boy has nothing wrong with him. He comes out here to the workshop because he likes these young people.' All the years they have wasted! Once you realize a person does have some mental or physical limitations, you must say to yourself, 'Yes, this person has some limitations, but let's work with the assets they have.'

"A real disappointment we sometimes have is when we have trained someone for a job, found an employer, and the parent has said, 'No, my boy (or girl) is not yet ready.' They are overprotective, or they do not care to disrupt a schedule they have built around this young person. For example, instead of coming to the workshop from eight to four, the young person may be working from seven until two.

"A lot of these changes in routine mean changes for the home helper, or helping people, and sometimes problems must be surmounted. The big one may be transportation.

"Yesterday I had a girl walk in that we had placed at Morrison's Cafeteria about a month ago. She came back to visit today. Another was placed in the housekeeping department of a local store. She also comes back, and in a sense it's like a family reunion. The housekeeping-department girl had a letter from her employer, who had been ill, commending her for her taking over and handling her work in the employer's absence.

"Workshops like this one give the people work matched with their abilities and challenge them. They start off with very simple contracts and progress to somewhat more complex contracts such as disassembling phones and sorting the parts according to type and color. There is a good deal of decision making here, for there are five different handsets and fourteen colors.

"Boys and girls enter from 16 up. The average age is 25, and they can stay as long as there is no outside placement. These young people have a right to realize their potential and achieve just like anyone else."

5
Normalcy in the Family

The most difficult word to define in our language must surely be "normalcy." None of us are certain what it is, but we begin to worry if we think we don't have it in our lives.

What did people do before there were surveys that would tell them whether their life was "normal"? Some were probably happy and did not know they should be unhappy. Now we read that there are certain basic needs that must be met if we are to be happy and lead a normal existence.

This may create as many problems as it helps to solve, but you are not so interested in theorizing at this moment. You know you have problems, and you are seeking to solve them. You will want to join your local Association for Retarded Citizens (ARC) and become part of a support group.

Problems in themselves are not abnormal. They are part of most people's lives, and those who have none are the exception. Reading the Bible, we discover one life after another with burdens. There is great inspiration to be found in this book, and if you have gone without *really* reading it for many years, you will find it speaking to your needs in a new way. You will find inspiration for overcoming difficulties. You will find the comfort and strength of a living Lord.

But you may ask, "Where is He in my own life tonight?" He is there. And, as the words in Mahalia Jackson's song assure us, "He may not come when you want Him, but He's right on time." When do you want Him? If you are like the rest of us, you want Him at the first sign of a cloud on your horizon. And, as we are enveloped in that frightening darkness, we cry out. As we read the Psalms there is one promise after another that He will hear us and *act*.

If we are to come out on the other side, we will rely on those promises. And as we live one day at a time, or even each hour of a day, we see so many indications that God is helping us. One contemporary song says "Thou shall not go down but through"; another, "Jesus was there all the time"; and you will find that He was!

Are you in control of your life? No, of course you are not, nor are any of the people around you. They are suffering silently, sometimes rebelliously. But there is strength and comfort to be found in religious music. If you haven't played it before, start. This is no time to feel foolish about it. Select records or tapes you like.

Several songs I have found most helpful are recorded by Evie, Chuck Girard, the Sharrett Brothers, and you will find your own. Play them when you are doing your housework or simply as a background to your days and nights. The words will enter your subconscious. They will become part of you—these affirmations of hope and life and the Lord's presence. They will renew you and bring organization out of the chaos created by pain and despair. Do you recall reading of the calm that descended upon Saul when David played for him?

The steps of psychology have much to offer, but only if we are standing on God's promises and the Holy Spirit is giving us the discernment to recognize the areas where we must brook no discouragement. Without the comfort of the Holy Spirit, there are many situations in which we will become bitterly discouraged—circumstances in which we are tempted to despair.

By the power of the Holy Spirit we will find strength to overcome discouragement: "I will pray the Father, and He will give you another Counselor, to be with you forever" (John 14:16). "May the God of hope fill you with all joy and peace in believing, so that by the power of the Holy Spirit you may abound in hope" (Romans 15:13).

It is faith that turns the wheel, and as this happens, we perceive where we must press on and work for greater progress in our relationship with the individual who needs help and with our families. The word of God, as it comes to us through the Bible and through sacred songs, begins to clear our minds, lifting us from the morass of despair and depression.

The problem that now looms so large can actually become a launching pad of growth for each member of the family. Faith and acceptance are contagious. You will begin to see your thoughts of martyrdom as an insidious form of self-pity. As the strength of the Lord flows through you, duties once done painfully lighten and are performed with love. One day, if people should say, "I don't know how you do it," you will truly wonder what they mean.

Yet loving people are by no means doormats. You will want to take care that you are not manipulated by the disabled or retarded individual just as you would if it were any other member of your family. Christ looked upon much suffering and tried to alleviate it, but there were times when even He needed periods of rest. You will need the renewal of *alone time*, also.

The most devoted helpers should also give time to the needs of the normal members of the family. Sometimes there appears to be a conflict, but these needs must be balanced and fulfilled without guilt. A husband and wife may decide to go off for weekends alone occasionally, to visit friends or to take part in a religious retreat—all renewing activities.

Once, I heard a young girl say, "All my father's time has been given to Jamie. Each time he comes home, he brings him a gift. Why am I penalized for being normal?" Our natural sympathy can run away with us, and when this happens the imbalance distorts the lives of others in the family. We who are helpers must be watchful so that, in caring for a broken person, we do not create other broken individuals and situations.

In the final analysis, normal people are those who are able to love and give, not to just one member of a family, but to others as well. Helpers who are able to express these qualities to the people around them are best able to create the atmosphere for a *normal* family life.

A balanced family life is incredibly difficult to achieve

when one individual presents problems involving special care, time, and attention. It is so easy for the full-time helper and other members of the family to become resentful, discouraged, or frustrated. The right church and the right pastor are of utmost importance. Your prayer life and fellowship life are critical.

If you are not in a supportive Christian fellowship under strong spiritual leadership, I would urge you to find this for yourself and your family. It is more than just supportive for you. It can be your very lifeline to a comfort and strength from God that you did not know was possible to receive.

You may already have this sort of fellowship, or you may not find it immediately. In any event, the following guidelines should be seriously and prayerfully applied to your life. They are all for the purpose of allowing the Lord to comfort and strengthen the inner person through the Holy Spirit.

1. Teach Me—Dear Lord, grant me a teachable spirit.
2. Give Me—Discernment as to Your daily path for me.
3. Help Me—Understand what You are doing in my life so that I don't despair.
4. Turn Me—From vanity and false pride back to Jesus.
5. Reassure Me—When I have fears and doubts.
6. Revive Me—Refresh and hold me up during problems.

Remember, there are three persons in the Godhead, the Father, the Son, and the Holy Spirit. We are to seek a relationship with *all three.* Reliance on these relationships must permeate us and become a part of our lives.

Does it seem to you that your life will be extremely hard and drab from now on? Do you look back on mornings when you awoke with a sense of happiness and expectation? It can be that way again.

The key to joy and inner peace in the midst of pain is the presence of the Holy Spirit. He is ready at this very moment to enter and fill your life if you will open yourself to this third member of the Trinity.

6

Being Needed Draws Them Together

Jim is a tall, red-headed young man with a beard, eyes that smile, and a quiet courtesy about him.

"My wife Debbie had polio when she was two years old and has spent the last 15 or 20 years of her life confined to a wheelchair. Debbie is paraplegic in that two of her limbs are impaired, but not totally. She has the ability to stand up by locking her knees. She can push with her legs and therefore is quite capable of driving a car and doing many things most paraplegics cannot as far as moving from the bed to the chair or into her car.

"When I first knew her, she was living in her own apartment, driving her own car, and getting around quite well. I met Debbie when I began a study-release program at the community college where she was working. I might explain that this was while I was in prison six or seven years ago."

Jim was a high school dropout. In an effort to become independent of his family, he went out on his own, but he lost his job, found himself in the wrong crowd, and, in desperation over his money problems, he was caught breaking and entering.

"My life in prison was a big turning point. Debbie was working in the special services office. The other students would leave campus when their classes were over, but I was restricted to the campus until the bus came to take me back to the camp. So, I found myself with quite a bit of free time and would go to Debbie's office to talk.

"While I was at the prison, I could have visitors, and, other than my family, Debbie was about the only one that would come every week. I met Debbie in January of 1976 and we were in married in January of 1977. We both felt very sure that we were meant for each other. It wasn't love at first sight, but it grew in a very short period of time.

"The one key thing that draws us so closely together and really makes our marriage—we both feel—is the knowledge of being needed and being wanted by the other. I think she needs me for the same things every man feels his wife needs him for. One very important thing, I think our marriage is like anyone else's, but we have closer bonds. To me that feeling of being needed and being wanted is the one thing that is the strongest in our marriage, and the lack of that may be the number one reason so many marriages fail. One spouse leads the other to feel that they are no longer needed or wanted for one reason or another.

"In our marriage, she is dependent on me to a certain degree, but more than that is shared. There is great companionship and love. But the most important thing is that we both feel very strongly that our marriage and our union is an act of the Lord. Debbie is 10 years older, but she lived a very protected life, and there is something almost childlike about her loveliness. In a sense I am much more worldly wise. I have always wanted to help and feel needed, and I've achieved that feeling with her.

"The blessings that everyone has wished us during our marriage, success and not a tremendous amount of failure, we thank God for in our prayers together.

"In our marriage—like anyone else's—we have good times and bad times, we have disagreements and arguments, we have times when we get very frustrated with one another, but that's normal. As far as the effects of Debbie's disability on our marriage, we try to make the best of it.

"One additional thing draws us closer. I was diagnosed as a diabetic when I was 15 years old, so in a way, I'm disabled too. That gives her a feeling of being needed because she helps me stay in line with my exercise and medication, and I know she feels that I need her just as much as she needs me.

"I like to be beside Debbie when she stands up to transfer from the bed to the chair to give her a feeling of security. We do the grocery shopping together, and since we work for the same company, we go to work together. When I attend school at night she does volunteer work at a nursing home, simply going and sitting with the patients. This is a highlight in her life.

"The faith we share is very important, and I believe that the things which might be a burden to others are not to me because of the love I have for her."

7
'You Can't Go by Yourself

Daren is 14 and is a profoundly retarded Down's syndrome boy. He did not walk until he was six. He still cannot talk or be left alone. His three older brothers and sisters are normal.

"Had Rod and I not been Christian parents, I don't know how we would have handled it," says Jody, his mother. "Our faith has been the source of the inner strength that has poured through us. We have to be willing to allow God to break through to us and help us develop whatever our potential may be. You can't go by yourself in this world without the help and the peace you need. Self gets in the way.

"The first year it was the unknown that baffled us. After that year we began to seek help to handle it from day to day in prayer. These children and adults are such precious gifts; they teach us what love really is.

"There are many problems in trying to care for Daren's needs. Since he can't talk, I don't know what is wrong with him or where he hurts if he is sick or falls. From the very beginning you become frustrated because you don't understand how to solve communication and self-care problems. Daren will go to the sink if he wants water, but then he can't turn on the faucet.

"One doctor advised us to put him in an institution immediately. Another told us he would never walk; yet he is walking. I talked with one of these doctors and asked him to tell me Daren's assets and liabilities. He seldom referred to Daren in a manner that indicated Daren was a person. I said, 'Let's get off on the right foot. When you stop referring to him as a product or business situation, I'll tell you more about Daren. We are referring to a person.'

"We have tried to take advantage of every opportunity. The Center for Human Development here suggested that they could help him learn to feed himself, but he would have to stay there about three months. At that time he wouldn't eat for anyone but me. Of course, we didn't think anyone could take care of him but us. But we decided to try it, and for three months I took breakfast over there for him every morning at 7:30. Eggs, oatmeal, fruit, milk, or whatever he was eating at the time.

"Parents have to be willing to do this at an hour that may be inconvenient. Finally, it was a black woman who taught him how to feed himself. She was fantastic! And Daren made more progress, for he eventually let other people feed him.

"I was really grateful for the help this facility gave me. As soon as parents find out their child is not functioning normally, they should get in touch with a good diagnostic center. You've got to stay abreast of what's going on. We are working now to get legislation through for group homes for the severely retarded.

"Our older children have accepted this situation, but my advice is not to center your family life and your attention around that one exceptional child. We tried to divide our time among the older children, and we went to all their games even if we had to take Daren. We made a point of not letting him have all our attention. I think we realized early on that there was a difference between a problem and a situation. A problem can often be solved, but when the outcome is not in our hands, it is a situation. This is something we must handle every day. My husband and I have both pulled together, and his faith is just as strong as mine.

"Last spring my mother had broken her hip, Rod was in the hospital, and there was Daren to care for. One night I turned to a verse in the Bible in Psalms. It said, 'I am thinking of you constantly,' and I could just feel His arms about me. To feel this is to have a real commitment, as we do to our work and marriage."

Daren is in a year-round day program from nine to three at a center for the severely retarded. His mother has a part-time typing job outside the home. The summer Daren was 14 his parents took advantage of a respite care program to take a vacation trip to Florida. The year before, it was the West.

"We have the support of family and friends," says Jody, "and God has said He will see us through."

8
Why Did This Happen to Me?

The man in church a few rows ahead of me had white hair and a pleasant, almost childlike face. He appeared to be participating fully in the service, and yet there was something about him not quite like other people. His name was David, and his mother, Jane, shared what it was that makes David different.

"My David is 53. He has been a spastic since birth, but it was a full year before my husband, Andy, and I were really afraid that something was wrong with him. David was so slow to be able to handle himself. Our obstetrician died shortly after the baby was born, and we couldn't see his records or find out what went wrong.

"Right after David's first birthday I took him to a medical center. I wanted the truth, and I said, 'Tell me everything so I know how to face this.' When a problem confronts me I'm going to fight it. The child specialist turned to me and said, 'I'd never put a dime on his life. He won't live beyond 13 years.' I replied, 'While there is life, there is hope.'

"In the beginning I asked God, 'Why did this happen to me?' And then I turned around and said, 'Lord, I'm not questioning, I know there is a purpose.' It drew my husband and me closer together, and I think that was the purpose. We had always been close, but we were even more so when we had a problem. We started preparations for David's future immediately after we knew the situation. Each month we put money into a trust fund for him.

"I began to train David patiently but strictly, encouraging him to live up to standards he can handle, and I gave him lots of praise. My faith became stronger as I went along, and I believe the Holy Spirit gave me the faith that I began to have. As David grew older, our pastor was very interested in him, and he used to take him to church picnics and ball games and always saw to it that David sat between him and his wife at their potluck dinners.

"When I talked with him he would say, 'I am convinced that he is very much with the Lord, and I can see God doing his work through David.' David enjoyed going to church and had a multitude of friends there. During the time I was growing up, my own parents seemed to enjoy going to Sunday school and church, and although they never forced religion on us or said it was a must, we could see how much it meant to them. I am sure David has felt this with us as I did with my own parents.

"I have been so grateful for his well-being, and many times I have thanked the Lord for the capabilities David has. He cuts the lawn, cares for his own room, and makes his bed. Since I am a widow now, I keep this big house for him, and he in turn helps me when it's needed. My husband had Parkinson's disease and high blood pressure, and for the last 15 ye of his life I spent much time with him. He lost his speech and then one of the strokes took his eyesight.

"Sometimes I would say, 'Lord, why this burden on me? Haven't I been a good person?' At one time I felt I was being punished. I never got the answer to all the whys. Finally, I said, 'If this is Your will, Lord, I'll obey.'

"I feel I have some very happy memories. The Lord has bestowed—and is still bestowing—many blessings on me. David and his brother are six years apart, and his problem did not embarrass his older brother. For years he has taken guidance with such a good spirit. I am almost 78 now, but am within walking distance of my older son's house, and David is a real comfort to me in the loneliness since my husband's death. I suppose it has been years since I really asked the Lord, 'Why?'

"There has been much happiness in my life along with some very hard times, but through it all my faith has held me up."

9
It's Easy to Be Overprotective

Looking back, Janice, the mother of 12-year-old Leane, sees that there are many things she might have done differently, "but it's so easy to be overprotective."

"From the time our little girl was born she was sick continuously. Leane had a heart defect, and it was natural that we began to shelter her right from the beginning. We never took her out in crowds; we didn't even take her to the church nursery until she was four years old, for we were always fearful of exposing her to infection.

"What really brought me out of my shell was when we decided to take her to the kindergarten here for retarded children. Leane was three and a half, but she was still on baby food and a bottle, although she was potty trained. The first day she was there, they took the bottle away. They introduced her to soups with solids in them like meatballs and noodles. She is 12 now but still eating the same thing. When we put good things on the table and ask her to try them, she says no, and she gags if we try to get her to taste them. She eats only about six things over and over. I think we should have been much more firm in insisting she form better eating habits.

"We keep working with her, but I believe if I had sought continuing professional advice from the time Leane was born, she would have made so much more progress. It has always been hard for me to apply some of the same methods I would have used with a normal child; yet I know now that is what I should have been doing all along.

"She still wets four or five times during the night, although she does well with bladder control during the daytime. She still cannot tie her shoes, but she can brush her teeth and change into her nightgown. I always help her put on her school clothes, but I think if we gave her a little more time and would be more patient in the morning, Leane could soon be putting on her own clothes completely.

"It was only last April, when she was 12, that we started letting her ride the bus to school. I had always thought I could just as easily take her and pick her up. But she enjoys riding the bus and is doing just fine. She even began to seem more independent. Somehow, I didn't think I could let her try it, and it was my problem instead of hers. I let her stay outside by herself, but we check on her, for we live on a busy street, and I feel it's important to watch her.

"At her school there is a class for the trainable mentally retarded, and Leane is now reading on a second-grade level. I've been so pleased to learn that she has started to help in the cafeteria, and I think she could help more at home. We are showing her how to do simple tasks like vacuuming, folding towels, and clearing the table, which we could have done much sooner.

"We have changed churches to one that has a class for mentally retarded children, and she enjoys it so much. The teachers and people at this church have been wonderfully kind and supportive. Through both this class and the kinder-garten, I have met other parents with mentally retarded children, and I don't know what I would have done if I had not been able to really open up to them and share our mutual problems. I saw that they had made it, and that I could make it too.

"My eight-year-old son asked me why Leane had to be mentally retarded, and I replied, 'That is the way she was born. We don't have the answer as to why, and there is nothing we can do about it. We love her the way she is, just as we do you.' We are together so much that he and Leane receive about the same attention. We put about the same amount of money into their gifts. We have tried very hard to treat them about the same. If both get into trouble, their punishments are similar, a spanking or being deprived of some small pleasure.

"At first, Eric, my husband, accepted this a lot better than I did, for he has a strong faith. We found that the things that had worried or irritated us before this happened don't even bother us anymore. There are too many other things to think about. Eric and I love each other a great deal, and it has made our marriage even stronger."

10
When the Helper Must Let Go

In his room down the hall from me my 17-year-old boy is watching television. At about 10 o'clock he will turn it off, sit on the floor and color for awhile before getting ready for bed. He will come soon to show his picture to me and ask, "How you like it, Momma?" And I will say, "It's good, David."

Today has been just like many others, except that it rained, and we could not go out and play catch with his baseball. While I was frying chicken, David came in to the kitchen and patted me on the back. "You're my best momma," he said, as he has so many times. I replied, "Thanks, honey, you're my best boy." And for me there won't ever be any other boy, because he is my only son.

He really has been the best, although some people might not understand that. David is a Down's symdrome, or mongoloid, youngster. His IQ has varied in tests from 47 to 53. If I'm feeling blue, David senses it and will ask, "You all right, Mother?" or, "Momma, please don't worry." Three years ago, when my husband and I separated, it never occurred to me that someday I would have to give up David.

Since then David, my daughter, and I have lived together. But he is now 17, and there are no friends for him in the neighborhood. Sometimes younger boys nine or ten years old will come to see him, but David is at once too mature and yet not quick minded enough for there to be real companionship. I sense that David is the one they come to see when there is no one else to play with. David treats them politely but with a certain lack of interest.

David is a help to me here in the house. He empties waste baskets, takes out trash, vacuums, and does reasonably well straightening the kitchen or picking up in the living room. He helps bring in wood for the fireplace or crushes papers to build the fire. He enjoys going to the store with me and brings in and puts up the groceries.

On the other hand, he may go outdoors in winter with his shirt sleeves rolled up and no jacket, or he may disobey me and go over too often to a neighbor's home where the father has played ball with him. When the doorbell rings, he dashes to the door, and if I were not here, he could open it to a stranger. If I were gone and he was alone and a fire started, he might be looking for the cat or dog while the flames spread.

Last Friday night I took him to the dance at his special school. He loves dancing, and when I led him up to a girl sitting on the sidelines, he held out his hand graciously and asked her to dance. At home he has danced while he watched people on television, and he's right in time with the music. But on this night his girl friend wasn't there, much to his disappointment. She is a sweet-looking young girl, and on one occasion I talked with her mother.

The next afternoon David wanted me to phone her, and I dialed the number for him. He told her that "Momma says she will take us to MacDonald's for lunch." "I always get a Star Trek meal," she said shyly. An hour later her mother called to say she couldn't go and that she thought their friendship had best be restricted to school. Of course, I respected her wishes, but David was crushed. "Why doesn't my girl friend's momma like me?" he asked for several days afterward.

Sometimes when we have driven along alone in the car, I have looked over at David and seen tears sliding down his cheeks. "What's the matter, honey?" I ask. "I'm thinking about my girl friend." "What about your girl friend?" "I want her to come live with us." Such grown-up longings and yet this is the same youngster who wants me to come into his bedroom at night and sing "Jesus Loves Me" to him and join him in his prayers.

Now his sister is in college, and the time approaches when she will be spending the summers away and cannot be counted on to be with David if I am not here. Temporary care is available, but nothing on a prolonged basis, for the group homes that are all too few in my city of Charlotte, N. C., are filled, and the waiting lists are long.

The closest home where we might be able to send him is five hundred miles away in the city where his father lives. I know he enjoys other young people and will like seeing his father more often. But there is no way to describe the pain in letting him go. It hurts as though one of my limbs were severed to know that I won't be hearing David say "You're the best, Mom," to see his room empty, to not have that figure in his orange ski jacket streak out of the house at the last minute to go with me on an errand.

I know he will have companionship and the full-time supervision he needs. I also remember very well a family who had a retarded youngster who grew up in the days when there were no group homes at all. Both his parents died. His sister moved out of town, and he lived in a gigantic old house all alone. What sort of meals did he eat? Who took care of him when he was sick? Who kept his clothes clean and mended? I really don't know, but I'm sure David would not be able to exist without some intelligent people to help and supervise him. He is completely unable to handle his own money.

When David was born and we learned he was a Down's syndrome child, the pain was incredible. Now, after years of loving him, there is another sort of anguish to endure, and I want those 17 years back. I want to rebel at the agonies of life that can't be changed or prayed away but must be accepted. And only the Holy Spirit can help me heal inside and wipe my tears away.

Resources and Rights

Court rulings that institutionalization for retarded people is unreasonable separation from society have resulted in the establishment of "group homes" in some states. Here up to 12 persons live in a home environment under supervision. They are given training in practical skills for daily living, personal hygiene, grocery shopping, check writing. Your state or regional mental health center can provide information about the location of both group homes and sheltered workshops.

Financial and medical assistance (Medicaid) are available for retarded children and adults under the Supplemental Security Income Program (Title XVI of the Social Security Act). Depending on the size of your community, there are some free services—transportation, training in self-help skills, day care and sitters—available through state social services programs (Title XX of the Social Security Act). Contact your state welfare agency.

Recent federal legislation affecting the retarded includes:

- —Education for All Handicapped Children Act of 1975—a program that helps state and local education agencies finance special education. It guarantees every handicapped child the right to a free and appropriate education.
- —Vocational Rehabilitation Act of 1973—provides vocational training for handicapped adults with employment potential.
- —Developmental Disabilities Assistance and Bill of Rights of 1975—calls for statewide planning for services and provides direct services to individuals in two

of four priority areas. States may choose from the following areas: social developmental; community residential; case management (following through on individual program plans); and infant services.

For general information on services available, contact your state or local chapter of the Association for Retarded Citizens or write the National Association for Retarded Citizens, 2709 Avenue E East, Arlington, Tex. 76011.

Information is also available from your own state offices. Write to the developmental disabilities council, protection and advocacy agency, department of education (or county board of education), or office of vocational rehabilitation in your area.